IMAGES OF GOD

Finding the Lord in Ordinary
Objects and Everyday Events

IMAGES
OF
GOD

LEO HOLLAND
Foreword by George Martin

AVE MARIA PRESS ◆ *Notre Dame, Indiana 46556*

© 1984 by Ave Maria Press
Library of Congress Catalog Card Number: 84-72318
International Standard Book Number: 0-87793-276-X

Photography:
    John David Arms, 22; Cleo Freelance Photo, 92;
    Bob & Miriam Francis, 52; David R. Hiebert, cover;
    Phil Kaczorowski, 12; Theo Robert, 32; Vernon Sigl,
    42, 62, 72, 82.

Cover and text design: Katherine A. Robinson
Printed and bound in the United States of America.

===To===
Joseph M. Bagiackas
for vision and encouragement

Acknowledgments

It is not for an author to claim divine inspiration. But for me this book is more a product of God's influence than my own creative talent. On reading the final drafts of the manuscript, I was impressed by how much the words seemed to be something addressed *to* my mind and heart, not something coming *from* them. I pray that God will use them to speak to readers' hearts in a personal and powerful way.

I am grateful to Eugene Geissler and Kenneth Peters, my editor at Ave Maria Press, for important guidance and advice at critical points in my work. Also to Frank Cunningham for believing in the concept and spirit of the book. Special thanks to Jane Dutro for typing assistance. Above all, my gratitude to my wife, Peg, for her sustaining wisdom and patience.

Leo Holland

Table of Contents

Foreword

Images of God is a book of vision. Not a book of visions like Ezekiel's chariot of God or John's new Jerusalem; it is rather a book of vision, of insight, such as Amos had when he saw significance in a plumb line or a basket of ripe fruit. In visions, we see what is normally hidden from our eyes; with vision we see meaning in what is right before our eyes. Amos saw the plumb line as a symbol of God judging his people and finding them wanting. Amos saw that God's people were on the verge of destruction, just as the ripened fruit was on the verge of going rotten.

So too Leo Holland looks at ordinary objects and everyday events and sees in them glimpses of God. He looks at the fine craftsmanship of a table and sees it as an image of our being crafted by God, polished until we become a thing of beauty in his hands. He watches a lizard watching him, and sees it as a parable of God's unblinking vigilance. This is vision: to see significance in the ordinary, to recognize that the world around us is filled with images of God.

Many of the shorter parables of Jesus are similarly matters of vision: to contemplate a tiny mustard seed and learn from it a lesson about

9

the kingdom of God, to watch a poor woman searching for a lost coin and see in her search God's search for us, to learn from a grapevine something about our dependence on Jesus. Jesus tried to give his followers the vision to understand such ordinary things as signs of a more profound reality.

It is therefore fitting that each image of God that Leo Holland proposes for our reflection is illuminated by a passage from scripture. The words of Jesus should open the eyes of our minds to the deeper meaning that lies in the everyday and commonplace. Our vision must ultimately become his vision, for to see through his eyes is to truly see.

Our seeing should lead naturally to prayer. Not prayer as if we were asked to compose a prayer for some solemn occasion, but prayer as we would naturally talk with a loved one about something important that we had just noticed. There is a graceful flow from each day's scripture text and image to reflection and prayer.

The hope of any author is not merely to share his or her unique vision, but to help others discover and sharpen their own vision. Hence *Images of God* provides not merely 40 days of meditation, but an example of what each of us can and should do in searching for the foot-

prints of God in our world. Each of us is sur-
rounded by countless images of God, if we but
have the vision to see their significance. We can
be grateful to Leo Holland that his *Images of
God* is itself an image of our discovery of God.

George Martin

1

*Do not, then, surrender your
confidence; it will have great
reward. You need patience to do
God's will and receive what he
has promised.*

Hebrews 10:35-36

Image: The Chinese Table

We were in Hong Kong shopping and I was
fascinated by a small table in jade green
Chinese lacquer. The color and shading were
exquisite. The impression of depth in the table
top was uncanny; it looked cool, deep and inviting.

The old Chinese merchant patiently explained that the effect was created through the
patient application of 12 coats of lacquer. Each
coat was finely sanded and hand rubbed. I
noted that it was a time-consuming process.

"It is the only way," he said. "Here we
make time for what is necessary." I gathered
that beauty and craftsmanship were a necessary
part of his life.

Jesus said clearly that he is the only way to
the Father. He generously lived out his love in
sacrifice to show us in what that way consists.
His way, like Chinese craftsmanship, takes time,
commitment and patience.

The fine sanding of penance and self-denial and the hand rubbing of worship and praise can, in time, create a soul of depth and beauty—cool and inviting, even to God.

Prayer:

Father, as I begin this holy and profound season, let me be always conscious of the journey on which I now embark. Let me see the road clearly. Let me anticipate with strength and vigor the demands I want to make on myself.

Fill me with wisdom and knowledge to see the truth underneath the daily observances. Let me grow in joy, victory and closeness to you so that sacrifice, fasting and self-denial do not become ends in themselves.

Let me not quibble. Let me see everything as a close walk with Jesus, a special time with him, an opportunity to be a true and loyal friend to my Lord.

2

From this time on, many of his disciples broke away and would not remain in his company any longer. Jesus then said to the Twelve, "Do you want to leave me too?" Simon Peter answered him, "Lord, to whom shall we go? You have the words of eternal life. We have come to believe; we are convinced that you are God's holy one."

John 6:66-69

Image: **Being Available**

Jesus awakens on a grassy slope near Jerusalem. As the first light dawns, the apostles begin to stir; one by one they awake and stretch and yawn. Another day is beginning in their walk with the Master.

It is overwhelming to realize that the apostles were so simply and totally available to the Lord. Despite their limited grasp of his full identity, they followed Jesus and were with him night and day.

When you awake in the morning, Jesus is also there, fully present to you just as he was to the apostles. Like them, you may not fully understand his plan for your life. You can ignore him but that does not diminish his presence or his rightful lordship over your life.

The apostles were ready to move on with Jesus—to not only be available to him but to be faithful—to persist in love and service.

When you awake tomorrow, look around and you will see Jesus stirring, too, ready to lead you through a day in which he can use you, your work and your talents for his purpose.

Prayer:

Dear Lord Jesus, why am I so blind? Your invitation of love and mercy extends down through the ages to all men and women of every time and place. We are all called to intimacy and union with you.

Give me the grace, Lord, to greet you in the morning, to be close to you all day and to lie down to sleep at night with your name on my lips. No matter how bruised I may be, how confused or discouraged by events, keep me as your weak but willing instrument. Fill my heart with courage and loyalty.

3

*There was also a certain
prophetess, Anna by name,
daughter of Phanuel of the tribe
of Asher. She had seen many
days, having lived seven years
with her husband after her marriage and then as a widow until
she was eighty-four. She was constantly in the temple, worshiping
day and night in fasting and
prayer.*

Luke 2:36-37

Image: Satan in the Desert

Imagine a desert scene. It's hot and the sun
beats down on you without mercy. You are
tired and alone and your canteen is now less
than half full. You are on the edge of survival.

Satan trails you with a malevolent eye,
stalking you relentlessly, waiting for you to give
way to loneliness, fatigue, fear and thirst.

You realize that you are being strongly
challenged and your competitive spirit rises. In
a moment of righteous anger, you rip off your
canteen, and turning, empty it at Satan's feet.
Snarling, he walks away shaking his head and
muttering, "What can I do with someone like
that?"

This little scene reminds us that each of us has the power within, through God's grace, to receive Satan's challenges and to rout them through embracing prayer, fasting and sacrifice. Learn to savor the power in frequent self-denial; it is one of the great joys of the Christian life to which you have a personal right as a child of God.

Prayer:

Jesus, give me the heart of Anna the prophetess that I may become a person of prayer and fasting. Teach me to live a prayerful life and a disciplined life. Lord, let me taste the sweetness of sacrifice on my tongue. Lead me, teach me, and guide me to follow you and to imitate your love for our Father.

4

O Timothy, guard what has been committed to you. Stay clear of worldly, idle talk and the contradictions of what is falsely called knowledge. In laying claim to such knowledge, some men have missed the goal of faith.
1 Timothy 6:20

Image: The Sand Hills

The sand hills of the desert seem like eternal and immovable sentinels. But during the long desert nights the wind blows continuously and changes the shapes of these silent witnesses. Each morning they present a new array and a new configuration.

We are like those sand hills. We change and grow stronger or weaker. We are deeply affected by both good and evil.

Our faith is a strong shield, but the winds of the world continuously blow false values at us through all of the public media. Without daily prayer and careful discernment we can become changed every day into new shapes and forms which reflect selfish and materialistic ideas and values.

We need a healthy cynicism concerning the

spirit of the world and its pretensions, its empty promises and its superficial and destructive attractions. Know these winds for what they are and what they want to do to you.

Stand firm in your faith. Incorporate the ancient wisdom of God in every fiber of your being so that you stand immovable and strongly rooted in him. Avoid the fate of the sand hill.

Prayer:

Lord, deceptive and misleading winds blow around me. They are everywhere I turn. They chant a litany of half-truths and lies. They hammer incessantly from many external sources.

Within me, Jesus, your voice is so quick and calm, so full of peace. Lord, grant me time to listen. Direct my thoughts and attention inward. I want to be with you in the quiet inner bower of my soul. That is my source of strength, the hope of my heart. Thank you, Jesus, for the inner light of faith.

Images of God

5

*No test has been sent you that
does not come to all men.
Besides, God keeps his promise.
He will not let you be tested
beyond your strength. Along with
the test he will give you a way
out of it so that you may be able
to endure it.*

1 Corinthians 10:13

Image: Flight of the Feather

I stood underneath an oak quietly observing a
robin feeding her young. As I watched, a small
feather slowly floated down from the nest area
where two branches grew together.

I was impressed by the long time it took for
the feather to reach the ground. The feather
seemed to be descending as if stepping down little stairsteps in the air. It moved erratically and
sometimes would swoop upwards for a moment
and then continue its slow descent.

The descent of some people into serious
habitual sin is like the downward flight of that
little feather. As the wind gently supports the
feather, God's grace supports them in virtue and
in a taste for what is right. But they reject the
promptings of grace, turn away from God's help
and support and tumble into willful disobe-
dience to God's law and love.

Seeking satisfaction in sin brings futility and anger. Sin always reveals itself ultimately as a lie and a deception.

Jesus loves us and provides the necessary adequate graces for every situation. Through his grace we can avoid the flight of the feather and glide on the eternal victorious wind of the Holy Spirit.

Prayer:

Jesus, you were tempted in the desert. You know how artful Satan can be. You know my human weakness and my fragile heart. Strengthen me, O Lord, with your divine life. Give me your heart and mind so that I can see the darkness of Satan, however cleverly camouflaged.

Give me strength not only to recognize and reject sin, but to be so close to you that my rejection of temptation is immediate and instinctive.

6

*I want you to be wise in regard
to what is good and innocent of
all evil.*

Romans 16:19

Image: The Marbled Steak

A marbled steak, with the fat and meat closely
intertwined, was once considered highly
desirable. But in the light of current medical
theory regarding the effects of cholesterol, it is
now regarded with some suspicion. Some people
avoid it entirely; some eat it occasionally; others
throw caution to the wind and eat it whenever
they please.

Our environment is also marbled with good
and evil opportunities. They are frequently intertwined and not always presented clearly. We
cannot entirely avoid evil. Sin is not like a bit of
food that we can pass up. It is not totally outside us. The root of sin is within.

We need strong inner convictions and
habits of virtue to sniff out sin in its various
sugar coatings and to develop in ourselves what
the medieval theologians called "res
gestae"—the taste for what is right.

Prayer:

Lord Jesus, you gave your life for me. In the

mystery of your divine love my life takes on eternal meaning and dignity.

Fill my heart and mind with your Holy Spirit so that I may have an active and eternal hunger for goodness and for you.

I reject all evil. I reject Satan and all of his works. Fill me with yourself, Lord, so that there may be no room in me for anything but you.

7

> *"Not as man sees does God see,*
> *because man sees the appearance*
> *but the* LORD *looks into the*
> *heart."*
>
> 1 Samuel 16:7

Image: A Remarkable Boy

Barry was 11. He was the youngest son of dear
friends. Strong, forceful and imaginative, he
met life head on. One day we climbed one of
the highest mountains in the Shenandoah Na-
tional Park. Barry and my son Jim went up the
rocks like mountain goats; they got to the peak
before the rest of us and Barry laughed with
delight. He was an active and healthy boy but
there was something special about him.

One year, on Mother's Day, he quietly cut
some flowers from the family garden and took
them over to a neighbor's house. He knocked on
the back door. The woman at the house knew
him, "Barry, why are you giving me these
flowers?" He said, "Well, it's Mother's Day and
I know you don't have any children and, well, I
just thought you might like them." She called
his mother later and they shared their joyful
astonishment at this little boy who possessed
such a mature and perceptive heart.

Prayer:

Father, I carry in my breast a heart that is too often hard and cold, closed and fearful, unwilling to risk, to reach out.

Fill me, Lord, with strengthening grace and the liberating power of your Holy Spirit so that my heart, like Barry's, can reach out and bring your love to others.

8

But the path of the just is like
shining light,
that grows in brilliance
till perfect day.

Proverbs 4:18

Image: The Alabaster Sheet

The long thin sheet of white alabaster was
beautiful and translucent. My little daughter
held it up and exclaimed, "See how the light
shines through."

We can be like that. We can become holy
and translucent. We need to cultivate virtue
and openness to God so that when his light and
grace come and enter into us, they can shine
through.

As Christians we, like Jesus, are truly for
others. God for his own reasons wants to reach
others through us. He wants his truth and love
acted out in our lives to the benefit and salvation of those he sends us.

He dispenses his grace and truth no matter
what we do. It can come out horribly distorted
and fuzzy if we are not surrendered to him, living a life of virtue and love.

Prayer:

Lord Jesus, you bless me daily. Your love pours

over me like a summer shower. I feel warm and secure in your care. My heart is filled with love and thanks.

With all of your goodness to me, why is my faith so rooted in my own needs? Jesus, help me to move outward. Let your love flow freely through me to others. Teach me to seek out the hurting and the needy. Do not let your grace curdle in me. Help me to let your light shine through.

9

You must know that your body is a temple of the Holy Spirit, who is within—the Spirit you have received from God. You are not your own. You have been purchased, and at a price. So glorify God in your body.

1 Corinthians 6:19-20

Image: **Authenticity**

There is something uniquely warm, attractive and satisfying in the human person. Facial expression, the glint in the eye, laughter, the flash of teeth, expressive body movement—they all delight us in their individuality, power and dynamics.

We owe our neighbors the privilege of receiving our real selves. We owe them directness, honesty and spontaneity.

To conceal the love, wit and wisdom that God has gifted us with is a form of sinfulness. To repress, distort or hoard God's gift keeps it from its proper and intended use. We can cooperate with God or we can dig in our heels and frustrate the working out of his design in us.

God wants to build us in strength and power to reach out to others—to love, to comfort, to counsel. The strength is his—he wants us to use his gifts—to open our hearts and hands with joy unafraid and strong faith.

Prayer:

Lord, I swing from arrogance to self-pity and back again. Never able to see myself as I am—as you see me. My self-image is distorted by fear and lack of confidence.

Jesus, stabilize my soul. Grant me the kind of self-knowledge and humility that bring peace and strength. Fill me with your power so that I am not a burden to others but a help in bearing their burdens.

10

*My brothers, count it pure joy
when you are involved in every
sort of trial. Realize that when
your faith is tested this makes for
endurance. Let endurance come
to its perfection so that you may
be fully mature and lacking in
nothing.*

James 1:2

Image: Climbing Jacob's Ladder

During World War II, I remember on one occasion boarding a large ship from an LCT (Landing Craft, Troops). We climbed up ladders
made of heavy rope that hung limply over the
side of the ship; they didn't look especially hard
to climb.

Going up I was surprised at how difficult it
was to maintain my balance and keep up steady
progress as the ladder stretched in any direction
in which I placed stress. After considerable time
and exertion, I made it to the top with bruised
hands and tired arms and legs.

Our ascent to heaven is somewhat like that
World War II climb. As we move upward
toward God, we feel our human weakness pull-
ing us down. As we direct our effort and attention to God, we feel ourselves distracted by the

swaying and instability of our environment—the things we read and hear, the people we are sometimes with. As we fix our resolve to remain loyal and virtuous, we sometimes feel tired and exhausted from the forces of evil that attack us. So, swaying and slipping and lurching, we make our way to God, tired but confident in the overcoming and victorious love and grace of Jesus.

Prayer:

Lord God, you are the only one in whom I can fully trust. Yours is the only voice I can listen to with complete confidence. You are the source of my faith. Be with me, Lord, and shield me from the insincere and flattering word, from false attacks and ridicule.

Faithfully I want to make my way to you daily. I thank you for the good and holy companions you send to help me along the way. But I also need to overcome the negative forces in the world that press in on me. I need your help, Lord. I tire, sometimes I slip and fall. Thank you for being there to catch me, to help me, to set me right.

Images of God

11

*" 'Peace' is my farewell to you,
my peace is my gift to you;
I do not give it to you as the
world gives peace."*

John 14:27

Image: Shalom

Stephen was only 12, the youngest son of dear
friends and was slowly dying from an in
operable brain tumor. He was swollen from cor-
tisone and breathed from an opening that had
been cut into his throat. One eye was infected
and covered by a patch. He was having severe
difficulty in moving and using his limbs and
could no longer walk.

The memory that remains most clearly of
his months of infirmity is the image of his one
beautiful, blue eye. When anyone became
panicky about his movement or breathing, they
would look at him and be calmed by that eye of
peace. It said, "Shalom."

Stephen was calm and good-natured
through all of his ordeal. He was patient with
his father and others as if he were the older,
wiser head. He grew steadily worse. One day he
turned to us and said, "I know that I'm going to
die." His father said very carefully, "How do

you know this?" "God told me," he said simply and died peacefully shortly thereafter.

God was with Stephen in a special way all of his life. He was a blest boy, full of love for everyone. It was easy to believe that his peace during all that ordeal was God in him and with him in a deep way. The pain of losing him has dimmed, but the image of his patience and love remains bright and fresh and continues to encourage me and light my way.

Prayer:

Lord, strengthen me in your love. Lead me into prayer and sacrifice. Help me to turn away from the immediate, pressing and noisy clang of my thoughts and fears, and of the world around me.

Take me into your inner heart—past the gate, through the courtyard, into the very center of your love for me that I may taste your sweetness, holiness and purity. Teach me, like Stephen, to surrender everything to you that I may know your incomparable peace.

12

*The body is one and has many
members, but all the members,
many though they are, are one
body; and so it is with Christ.*
                    1 Corinthians 12:12

Image: **The Runners**

It had been a ten-mile race and we were
waiting patiently at the finish line for our
friends to come in.

I saw Fred and Bill from a distance. They
were alone and gaming out the last few hun-
dred yards in a head-to-head competition.
There was no one visible behind them. They
were running almost even, stride for stride. I
was surprised when, just 25 yards from the
finish line, they linked hands and came in
together, in an intentional dead heat.

Why?

I thought about what had happened, about
sportsmanship, about priorities and values,
about Christian love, and most of all, about
myself. I realized that I had seen something that
I wanted a part of, that I wanted to share in. I
realized that there is something better than the

personal desire to win an individual trophy. I realized what St. Paul means when he says we are to be saved together. He talks about being one loaf, and very frequently about being members of one body.

I knew that I had seen a human image of divine love that day, and I was glad and grateful that I was there.

Prayer:

Jesus, you died for all. You show no favoritism or partiality; you are fully present to each heart that turns to you. You show us clearly that we are to be saved, together, and that you love us, together.

Teach me, Lord, to see not only the members of the church but all men and women as members of your body. Give me the grace to reach out my hands to the angry, hurt, disappointed and alienated people standing outside the doors of your church.

13

*Lying lips are an abomination to
the LORD,
but those who are truthful are
his delight.*

Proverbs 12:22

Image: Matt

Matt is three, a beautiful grandson, a joy and a
great gift from God. On my birthday, he came
in from the yard as I was eating breakfast. He
had been playing in the flower garden and his
face and hands were covered with dirt. My
daughter Mary Ellen said, "Give Grandpa a
nice birthday kiss and hug." He gave me a
sweet and innocent kiss from that mouth
covered with garden dirt.

We frequently come to God like
that—covered with fatigue from our work, the
distractions of our environment, the demands of
family and friends. These earthbound con-
cerns—good in themselves—dilute our concen-
tration and limit our surrender to God in
prayer. God knows the limitations on our time
and energy but he also knows our hearts. He
knows that underneath the garden dirt of our
human distractions, our hearts are pure and
single-minded when they reach out in love to
him.

Prayer:

Jesus, you spoke the truth with love and compassion. Help me, Lord, to return that love in sincere and simple words from my heart.
Despite my distractions, my fatigue, my roving thoughts, purify my mind, my heart and my intention through your loving power.

14

*"Then you will know the truth,
and the truth will set you free."*
John 8:32

Image: **Free at Last . . .**

The large basket-like gondola and the huge colorful balloon above it were held fast to earth by ropes secured to large stakes in the ground. When the ropes were untied, the balloon rose rapidly and was swept forward by the wind.

It was exciting to see the swift and startling rise of the basket which swayed precariously. I was happy for my friends in the gondola but I also felt a sense of being left out, of missing their exciting adventure. It was clear that they were experiencing a special kind of freedom.

Attaining holiness means realizing a special kind of spiritual freedom. It demands that we cut loose from the things of earth and make ourselves totally available to God. Holiness is largely his work in us. We need to let go of our ego drives, our hyper-acquisitiveness and our excessive earthly ambitions and let God complete his work in us.

Others will desire and perhaps envy the excitement of our adventure with God. Some will feel a sadness at not sharing our experience. But all are invited; all can come; all are constantly sought by God. Human history is not so much our search for God but rather God's calling out to us.

Prayer:

Dear Jesus, I can scarcely contain my joy at your victory over sin and death. Thank you, Lord, for your grace, mercy and love during this Lenten time. Thank you for letting me walk beside you during both the dark and the victorious days.

My heart is saddened by the millions in bondage to sin. Save them, Lord, by your resurrection power. Show your light to the world. Illuminate every corner. Call all men and women to the good news that Satan's power was broken on Calvary and that your love and grace can heal and empower their lives.

Thank you, Jesus, for freedom and life eternal.

15

Take delight in the LORD,
and he will grant your heart's
requests.

Psalm 37:4

Image: Walking in God's Light

A debilitating nerve disease had temporarily paralyzed him. Once it was arrested, the therapists had to teach him how to walk again. He had to learn like a child; but with determination, he overcame his frustrations and succeeded.

God deals with us in somewhat the same way. We keep wanting things which we assume are good for us. We get discouraged when God doesn't answer our prayers and send these naturally good things along to us.

He then begins to change us and teach us new values. Figuratively, we learn to walk again. The good things we formerly wanted now seem less attractive or even undesirable. Like a child we need to learn what are the really good and valuable things, those which will help us to strengthen our character and expand our ability to love others with the heart of Jesus.

How kind and compassionate God is to

show us what the real desires of our heart are and then to provide them to us in such abundance.

Prayer:

Thank you, Lord, for changing my heart, for rebirth and renewal. Thank you for life in Christ.

Help me to fully reject all of my faults and sins. Show me the beauty and joy of prayer and fasting. Teach me how to rejoice in meeting the needs of others. Give me the strength to act apart from my own striving. Give me, Jesus, your heart and mind.

16

*The revelation of your words
    sheds light,
giving understanding to the
    simple.*

Psalm 119:130

Image: Simple and Direct

My wife and I were coming out of one of the beautiful old churches in Bucharest, Romania. The other tourists slowly boarded our bus. We tarried, chatting.

A little woman, very old, dressed in drab and worn clothes with the traditional kerchief around her head, came up to my wife and smiled sweetly. She took my wife by the hand and, looking intently into her eyes, said slowly and perfectly, "One, two, three, four, five, six, seven, eight, nine, ten." She smiled triumphantly with childlike delight at her "English" performance.

She obviously did not know or understand any additional English. My wife embraced her, kissed her lightly on the cheek, and we boarded our bus.

The image of that little old lady and her simple, pure-hearted direct love stays with me. We need some of that quality in our relationships with each other. We particularly need an unashamed desire to please others and the recognition of our need for their approbation and approval. Egotism, cynicism and distrust have overcome too many of us.

We also need some of that little old woman's childlike eagerness, openness and directness in approaching God. After all, he is our loving Father, Jesus is a brother who cares about us in an infinite way, and the Holy Spirit desires only to teach, comfort and sanctify us. What an invitation to directness and simplicity is our loving God.

Prayer:

Lord, the pursuit of knowledge can be a labor of delight. I can rejoice in learning. How good to use the mind you have given me.

Keep me, Lord, from vainglory and intellectual pride. Let me not use fine and intricate distinctions to justify my weakness and laziness. Save me, Lord, at all costs, from impatience and contempt for the simple and uneducated.

Help me to see daily my spiritual poverty and my mental limitations and to glory in your mercy, riches and goodness.

17

For you, O Lord, are good and
forgiving,
abounding in kindness
to all who call upon you.
Psalm 86:5

Image: Self-Inflicted Wounds

A man with a heavy-duty, industrial sander at-
tacked a corroded and pitted piece of metal.
The noise was horrendous. The sanding
machine brutally stripped the metal down to a
beautiful, smooth and shiny surface.

We sometimes become corroded and pitted
from the bitter acids of resentment, fear and
hostility. But God doesn't attack us in a brutal
way. His touch is sweet and light. He draws us
gently to himself and teaches us his ways
through healing our inner corrosion with his
love and concern.

Any brutality comes from ourselves, from
our stubbornness, pride and unwillingness to
change. We sometimes seem to want to hit bottom before we begin to repent and to change.
God respects our freedom and, as a result, he
has to watch us plummet to a bruising and
damaging fall. But he is always there, ready to
forgive and help us to rebuild.

Prayer:

O God, my heart aches with the knowledge of my unworthiness and the tenderness of your love. Of all your wonderful mystery, Lord, your forgiving love is the greatest enigma. Why, Lord, when I fall, do you stoop from your majesty to redeem me again and again? I praise and thank you and rejoice. Teach me how to serve you faithfully and to please you.

18

*For with you is the fountain of
life,
and in your light we see light.*

Psalm 36:10

Image: The Shimmering Tree

A tree shimmers reflectively in the light! The
same tree standing in the shadow of a fall day
presents a drab and dark image. Its colors are
flat and uninspired. But when God's light falls,
a magic change occurs. The beauty of the reds
and browns and golds is brought forth in shim-
mering and exquisite light.

We are like that tree. We also have a beauty that is already there, no matter how dimly
conscious of it we may be or how much we may
sometimes doubt its existence. The joy and the
victory of our salvation will shimmer gloriously
in the light of God's grace if we simply believe,
surrender and yield up to the life that streams
down continuously from him.

The tree can only reflect the light. We can
reach out to it, or reject it. We are active
cooperators and cocreators with God in receiving and manifesting his light to those he has
placed around us. How loving, kind and
generous is the God of light!

Prayer:

Father God Almighty, creator of all that is, I adore you and worship you and give you honor and glory. Give me the grace and wisdom to serve as a true and open channel of your word and love.

Teach me, Lord, to quietly accept your work in others through me so that I may be like the brook that humbly blesses the trout that glides through it in beauty and grace.

19

> *"This much have I told you while
> I was still with you;
> the Paraclete, the Holy Spirit
> whom the Father will send in my
> name,
> will instruct you in everything,
> and remind you of all that I told
> you."*
>
> John 14:25-26

Image: The Tumbleweed

The tumbleweed skitters erratically along the plains, at the mercy of every swirling eddy and crosscurrent. We are much like the tumbleweed, manipulated by the media and subjected to inconsistent and confusing communication from many political and religious leaders. Small wonder we often feel buffeted and lonely.

Jesus does not treat us like the wind treats the tumbleweed. He deals with us as free persons who possess dignity and value. He says, "I have chosen you, but you must choose me also. I will not force you to follow."

God generously provides a wind blowing in the right direction, in the person of the Holy Spirit, to teach, guide and direct us in making decisions in accordance with his law and love.

Prayer:

Holy Spirit, I want to place all of my talents, powers and activities totally under your divine protection and guidance. I want to speak your words and to manifest your power and purpose in my life.

Fill me with thoughts of heavenly things, of the excellence and majesty of our Father, of the love and merciful heart of Jesus. Move me to prayer and adoration. Teach me to understand God's ways and his word. Guide me and direct me so that when I walk I will not stumble or fall.

20

You have been told, O man,
what is good,
and what the LORD requires of
you;
Only to do the right and to love
goodness,
and to walk humbly with your
God.

Micah 6:8

Image: Surf and Sun

Even though it was mid-June I came out of the ocean surf somewhat chilled. The breeze didn't help. I ran up to the pavement on the seawall and stretched out on that hot and welcome surface. As I lay there I thought about the way the concrete absorbed and held the heat and how strange it was that the front of me was warm and comfortable while my back was still chilled.

We are something like that in our moral lives. The parts we give to God are warmed and comforted and protected by his grace and the infusion of his wisdom. Those areas we keep from him are cold, empty and lifeless—unprotected and in danger.

God does not honor a partially surrendered, compartmentalized life. We can't consecrate our family life to God, seek his protection and love in that area, and keep our business life separate, away from his law and love. He loves all of us and he wants all of us—heart, mind and body—fully surrendered to him so that he can be the Lord of our total life, as indeed he is.

Prayer:

In your mercy, Lord, you give me the grace and knowledge to meet every situation. You lead and inspire me. You teach and guide me.

Help me, Jesus, to carry always in my heart and mind an awareness of your immediate and personal love. Let it be like gentle unceasing music.

Let me not forget or tire or be led away to false attractions. Take all of my love, Lord, and all of my life.

21

*"I tell you all this
that in me you may find peace.
You will suffer in the world.
But take courage!
I have overcome the world."*
John 16:33

Image: **The Operation**

Coming out of the anaesthesia, I felt woozy; the room seemed to whirl around slowly. Gradually I saw the gentle smile of the nurse. She said, "It's all over, you're OK now; we're taking you back to your room."

At that moment, I felt a special admiration for the skills and talents of the doctors and nurses. Most of all I felt a strong sense of being cared for. It was a good feeling that stayed with me for days.

Our relationship with God is something like that surgical experience. We are finite; we sometimes see spiritual things dimly; we are afflicted with the internal warfare of fallen human nature. God, knowing our weakness, sends his grace to enlighten and strengthen us. He also sends gifted and loving people to help us on the way. Yet frequently we seem unable to correspond effectively with his grace. We awkwardly alienate some of the people whose help we so badly need.

Yet out of all of our striving and confusion we have moments of great peace and insight, comparable to coming out of the anaesthesia when we know with a special insight and clarity that God truly loves us and that he is protecting and guiding us always and everywhere. We know that we are cared for, in the highest sense.

Prayer:

Lord God, you are always with me in the fullness of your person and your power. And yet so often I miss you. I miss your word, your sign and your leading. How can I be so blind? How can I be so distracted?

Help me to be always open to receive you. Assist me, Lord, through your grace to cultivate a continuing sense of your presence and your authority over me and my life.

Images of God

22

*Put on the Lord Jesus Christ and
make no provision for the desires
of the flesh.*

Romans 13:14

Image: **Desert Resources**

We were far out on a desert hike and we sat
down in the meager shade of a large desert
plant for lunch. As I was munching on a sand-
wich, a lizard darted up out of the sand and
stared at me as if to say, "What are you doing
here in my domain?" I sensed he might enjoy a
bit of food so I tossed him a tuft of bread. He
took it and disappeared just as suddenly into the
sand.

I asked our hike leader, "How in the name
of God can any creature survive out here? There
is no water, no food and no shade from this
murderous heat." He laughed and said, "There
is an adequate supply of all these things for the
peculiar needs of these creatures. It is cool
underground; the plants harbor moisture. There
is a vast ecosystem at work here." I was surprised as he explained the complex interplay of
the environment.

People who have worldly success and
material goods in abundance sometimes over-

value their position, status and power. They have difficulty understanding how people without these resources can not only survive but prosper. They do not see the desert resources of people with character and religious faith. They don't understand the presence of God, the power of prayer and the consolation of religious sharing and love. They frequently don't understand the great strengthening and upbuilding that results simply from being in a large family of people who love and help one another. Build your life around desert resources and you will be ready for the hard day, the time of testing.

Prayer:

Jesus, you sought out the desert places and the mountaintops for prayer. You wanted to be free and alone with the Father.

Lord, I am drowning in sensory distractions and the care of many temporal things. Help me, I pray, to find the quiet time, the simple place, the detachment to be free and alone with you.

23

*For as the heavens are high above
the earth,
so surpassing is his
kindness toward those
who fear him.*

Psalm 103:11

Image: The Page on Top

The corners of the top page on my writing
tablet always curl up and there is really nothing
anyone can do to straighten them. It is very
frustrating. If the paper is smoothed out, it
simply curls back again. If it is bent back, it
creases. So periodically, the top page has to be
ripped off and a fresh new page started. This
familiar experience can serve to show how God
deals with us.

We sometimes curl up on the corners
because of sin. Too frequently a particular sin
can become a habit. When God, through his
grace and light, helps us to see our sin and turn
from it, it may unfortunately recur like the curl
in the paper because it has previously made
such strong inroads into our life.

God does not bend us back so strongly that
we crease. But he does permit the natural
results of our sinfulness to work their destructive

power in us. This is for us a way of learning. The results of our sin may be damaged health, a broken marriage, a loss of position or honor, or other serious defect.

God also does not abruptly tear off the stubborn and creased page and throw it away. Seeing our daily weakness and sinfulness, his patience, grace and love for us are infinite.

Prayer:

Lord, your love and kindness are precious to me. The immensity of your patience is awesome. But I also know that your justice is pure, holy and strong.

I want to live as a good servant, meriting your love. Help me, Lord, through prayer, fasting and service to root out sin in my life so that I may serve you in the best way.

Let your justice and mercy blend for me, Lord, that I may know, simply, your personal love.

24

*Faith is confident assurance con-
cerning what we hope for, and
conviction about things we do not
see. Because of faith the men of
old were approved by God.*
                        Hebrews 11:1-2

Image: **The Gray Horse**

I had been walking through the woods for near-
ly an hour and was tiring. I sat on the end of a
large log and enjoyed a brief rest. It was a hot
August day and the cool shadows of the deep
forest washed over me like a benediction. I sat
quietly as people do when they are hoping for a
sight of some wildlife. Nothing stirred. Suddenly
I saw a magnificent gray horse. He seemed dap-
pled but it could have been the broken sunlight
playing on him as he came toward me. I could
not see him clearly because of the trees and
underbrush and the pattern of shadows and
light.

I expected that he would be close to me in
a few minutes and I envisioned reaching out to
pet him and I remember thinking that I should
have an apple or something to draw him near.
Then suddenly he arched his neck, turned and
disappeared from sight.

God is something like that great horse. We see him from a distance dimly and we know that he comes to us always and everywhere but if we reach out to touch him, to make contact with him on the natural level, he is gone. We hope, sometimes ache, to hear his audible voice but he unites with us and deals with us on the spiritual and transcendent levels of wisdom, knowledge and inspiration. He preserves our faith and our need to trust in him.

I may never see that wonderful gray horse again, but I know that one day I will see my God face to face, forever knowing his peace and joy and love.

Prayer:

I believe, Lord; strengthen my understanding. I doubt, Lord; cast away my doubts. I love you, Lord; receive my love and let it return to me with your anointing.

Let my love and yours become a river that flows with power—first toward the seas of in- . finite love which you are—and back to me in my tiny cove.

I long for that day when I am united and consumed in the ocean of eternal love. Till then, love me, Lord, strengthen my faith, wash away my doubts.

25

So let us confidently approach the throne of grace to receive mercy and favor and to find help in time of need.

Hebrews 4:16

Image: Morning Mist

I awoke early. I felt the roll of the ship and heard the waves softly slapping against the hull. It was a bit of a surprise to wake up in the cabin of a yacht—not my usual environment.

I slipped into my clothes and went up on deck. We had anchored in a small cove where large trees grew out over the water. They cast deep shadows behind them.

A mist was rising from the water and moving toward me. In a short while it enveloped the whole ship. I wrapped a blanket around me and snuggled down into a deck chair. Soon a fish leaped out of the water and a heron sailed majestically by. I felt like an eavesdropper on nature. It was pleasant and peaceful.

The mist enveloped me gently. It covered everything like a gossamer blanket. I knew that the sun would soon dissipate it but now in the transitional world of early dawn it was a protective cover, screening, softening and beautifying everything.

I thought about God's grace and how all encompassing it is—like a universal and beneficent mist. No matter how great our sin or how isolated we may feel, God's grace creates for each of us a private pocket of forgiveness and reconciliation.

Prayer:

Thank you, Lord, for the knowledge of your forgiving heart and your strengthening and healing grace. We rejoice that your redeeming power extends to each of us fully, and without favoritism or partiality. Give us contrite and humble hearts.

26

*The night is far spent; the day
draws near. Let us cast off deeds
of darkness and put on the armor
of light.*

Romans 13:12

Image: **The Ripe Melon**

Many people have trouble guessing which
melons are the really ripe ones. They are often
surprised when they cut into one and find
perfect ripeness emerging much to their delight.

We are like that melon. God waits for us to
ripen. He watches us use our freedom in
responding to his truth and grace. He sees us
facing difficulties and trials—growing, learning
and building strength. He sees some of us reject
his truth and grace. He watches us falter,
weaken and turn to self-pity and wrong,
damaging solutions to our problems.

At some point the Lord must cut into the
melon, bringing our earthly lives to a close.
How tragic for those who have lived selfish,
low-risk lives. They remain green and stunted.
Equally tragic are those who have lived a life of
profligate self-gratification; they are overripe
and in many cases, rotten.

The man who has surrendered his life to

Christ, who has died to the world, who has remained in fidelity to God is at that perfect state of ripeness which delights the Lord throughout all eternity.

The choice is clearly ours; the balance is delicate. But Jesus leads, directs and guides. He is our assurance of salvation whenever God calls us home.

Prayer:

Lord, you know how artful is my hypocrisy, how clever my appearance of goodness, how tragic my compromise with the world and my ego drives. Even in my best moments I am like an unripe melon, flawed with pride and cunning.

Lord, I reject my weakness and my lack of simple honesty. I want to serve you with boldness and innocence. Fill me with your grace, Jesus. Teach me to pray, fast and serve others in humble ways, particularly those close to me. Make me a fool for Christ.

Images of God

27

Do you not know that God's kindness is an invitation to you to repent?

Romans 2:4

Image: The Fishing Line

It was late in the evening and we were going fishing the next morning. I went down to the basement storage room and hauled out my tackle box. I found the reels a little rusted and the fishing line was severely tangled but I went to work with enthusiasm. Soon the tackle box was cleaned out and the reels sanded and rubbed to a nice soft shine.

The snarled line was more formidable. I pulled and tugged and threaded the ends in and out for an hour, making little progress. There seemed to be hundreds of little knots working against each other. After a while I was able to salvage most of the line.

Later as I lay in bed I thought of the many knots in that tangled line and how much they are like our sins. Both are impediments to effective action, both are stubborn, complicated and difficult to eliminate. And both work together in a perverse way, one sin reinforcing another, just like the knots in the line.

We have to untangle our own fishing lines. But how great it is that Jesus can pick up the tangled line of our lives and if we only say the words, "Lord, forgive me, for I have sinned against you," he gives the line a little tug and miraculously—in a second—it falls straight and free.

Prayer:

Lord, you see me as I really am. Even my friends and those closest to me cannot see the full reality of my good and evil, my weakness and strength.

You know, Lord, more than I how deep and complex are my problems, how handicapped I am by the past. In your mercy, Jesus, heal me completely and deeply so that I can serve you in a better, stronger way.

28

After saying this, Jesus grew
deeply troubled. He went on to
give this testimony:
  "I tell you solemnly,
    one of you will betray me."
The disciples looked at one
another, puzzled as to whom he
could mean.

John 13:21-22

Image: The Russian Icon

Our Russian tour was highlighted by the colorful multiturreted church of St. Basil. I was
deeply impressed by a striking gold icon of
Christ that I saw there. The impression it made
stays with me.

The most notable feature of the icon was
the eyes—the Russian eyes—in that face of
Christ. They looked right through you; they
went deep into you in a way so piercing that
you flinched. I believe some people actually
stepped back.

Those eyes of Christ sent a communication
in three parts: "Brother—how can you do the
things you do—to me."

The brotherly salutation was a deep and
close revelation of the kind of love that Christ
bears for you and me, brother and sister. In

Moscow I felt stapled against the wall by his love. There was no way to keep an arm's length relationship with this Brother Christ.

The second part of the message brought horror and strong repugnance for my habitual sins. I realized for the first time how bad they really are. At that moment my every sin was so hideous I felt as though I couldn't breathe from the weight of all that evil.

The last part—"to me"—helped me to understand that my sins were bad, not in themselves, but in breaking faith with a brother who has loved me so much. To offend and dishonor the one true friend I had seemed so irrational I believed in that moment that I would never offend him again. I have sinned again, but I really believe my heart was changed and my relationship with Jesus is now closer and stronger.

Prayer:

Jesus, you know that I love you and want to please you in everything. Yet I sometimes fail you and betray your love for me.

Help me to be aware, to be wise, to be careful and to seek your grace in every situation. Help me not to be overcome by events and the hurly-burly of the day.

Come to me, dear Savior. Awaken my

heart so that I may be conscious of your presence and love through my every waking moment.

29

*"Today, if you should hear his
    voice,
  harden not your hearts as at
    the revolt
  in the day of testing in the
    desert."*

  Hebrews 3:7-8

Image: The Sun and the Rain

The night rain had made the ground soft and
mushy. There was no grass, only what seemed
to be a sea of mud.

As the water began to dry up, the ground
remained soft and malleable. A child walked by
and left a perfect set of footprints in the soft
clay. That soft surface it seemed was formed so
easily, yet the blazing summer sun would soon
bake it into hardness and immobility.

We are like that. God floods us with grace
to soften our hearts and open our minds to
receive him. We can, in those moments of openness and receptivity, take on the very heart and
mind of Christ. We are on the threshold of
realizing the kingdom of God within us and yet,
some people turn away. Like the sun baking the
clay they harden their hearts, rigidly adhering
to their own immediate desires and needs.

God sends his rain of grace upon us again and again. His generosity is infinite, yet our time here—in this life—is finite. We need to raise our heads, look up, open our dry and parched mouths to taste the holy rain from heaven that can replace our hearts of stone with hearts of flesh.

Prayer:

Dear God, self-will and sinfulness entice me to move farther and farther from you. Lord, do not let me drift away from your forgiving and healing heart.

Forgive me, Lord. Teach me, Lord. Change me, Lord, so that I may become and remain eagerly responsive to your holy will.

30

*"This is my Son, my beloved.
Listen to him."*

Mark 9:7

Image: God—Savior or Judge?

Years ago in a small Appalachian community at
a church picnic a young boy fell into the river
and was rescued from drowning by a local man.

Years later the young boy, now grown up,
committed a murder and was brought before a
judge for trial. His heart leaped with hope
when he saw that the judge was the man who
had saved him from drowning years before. But
the judge quickly clarified their relationship saying, "Things have changed. That day I was
your savior, today I am your judge."

Our image of God the forgiving and
redeeming Savior needs to be tempered with an
image of God the just and final judge lest we
presume on God's mercy.

Prayer:

Lord, you know how judgmental and self-
righteous I can be. How many times do I loudly
call for justice for others when justice for me
would be a calamity? Jesus, I am truly sorry for
having offended you, for failing you in any

way. You are the one I want to please and serve above all.

Lord, show me mercy and above all give me a heart of mercy for those around me. Teach me to forgive and forbear, and to love in patience and humility. Keep me from judging and judgment.

31

Here, then, is the message
we have heard from him
and announce to you:
that God is light;
in him there is no darkness.

1 John 1:5

Image: Light and Shadow

As I walked along a forest trail, I was surprised by the intense interplay of light and shadow. It was difficult to see things clearly. "Another assist from nature for natural camouflage," I thought.

The interplay of light and shadow can have negative effects as well. A high percentage of automobile accidents occur at dawn and at dusk when light and darkness are merging.

Our spiritual vision is also affected by the interplay of light and shadow, by the forces of good and evil that seem to emerge sometimes clearly, but always competitively. These opposing forces appear too frequently in subtle and indirect ways that leave one grasping for the reality behind the hype, the emotional pitch, the false logic, the surface appeal of evil, and unfortunately, the sometimes inefficient, insensitive, unintelligent and awkward presentation of the good.

Be prepared to sort out light from shadow. Carefully examine what is presented to you. Look behind the surface appeal. What is the bedrock, basic nature of the idea, event or presentation? What is at the root? Light or shadow?

Prayer:

Jesus, Lord of heaven and earth, I love and adore you. You alone know how confused and tentative I am. You alone know how often I move and act in compromise. You alone, Lord, see the darkness that I carry within me.

Send your light of love and courage into my deepest being so that I may speak your truth clearly and boldly in every situation.

32

"The Lord's hand is upon you even now!"

Acts 13:11

Image: Child of God

The attractive, well-dressed man moved swiftly through the crowded lobby toward the bank of elevators. As he passed a mother with a young boy, he gently placed his hand protectively on the child's head as he adroitly moved around them. His hand lingered lovingly for just a moment on the child's head.

This love for children seems to be a permanent human possession, a universal sign that erupts all over the globe in various public and private ways. The man in the lobby was reflecting this love in a specially dramatic and simple way as he moved on to his board meeting and business pursuits.

How much God the Father loves us. He created us, uniquely and specially, out of nothing, and sent his only-begotten son to redeem us from sin. He sent his Holy Spirit to sanctify and make us acceptable in his divine sight.

To those who pray and listen for his voice and seek his action in their lives, he sends a constant sequence of "love touches." He guides and directs, he comforts and heals, he inspires and exhorts. He places his loving hand on our head as he passes by.

Prayer:

Father God, when I contemplate my sins, my heart fills with fear. My guilt calls out for a stern hand and punishment. But your mercy and your loving call to salvation touch my heart with a loving response that casts out fear. Your hand upon me stills my fears and strengthens me.

Images of God

33

*I will bless the LORD at all times;
his praise shall be ever in my
mouth.*

Psalm 34:2

Image: The "Admirable" Snowman

I caught sight of a snowman on the front lawn
as I pulled into my driveway. His coal black
eyes glittered and seemed to be staring at me.
My children appeared from behind the
snowman where they had been hiding. They
were laughing with excitement at having surprised me with their wonderful creation.

I shared this time with them by signs of
wonder and admiration at their handiwork. It
was a pleasant interlude, full of love and joy,
one of those moments that make a father's life
worth living.

How much more our heavenly father
desires to share with us moments of love, joy
and victory. Why do we come to him only at
those times when we are beaten and bedrag-
gled, seeking mercy and comfort? We should
also look to him when we are in the winner's
circle—when we don't need him to solve some
problem—when we desire to share with him our
joys and victories. God should be God of all of

our lives, not just the dark moments of our deep needs.

Prayer:

Jesus, Lord of victory and joy, we rejoice with you today and join our voices with the multitudes in Jerusalem.

Lord, make this oasis during the Lenten season a time of special joy and upbuilding for those who are tired, discouraged and weakened. Let them share your strength and resolve, Lord. Let them walk beside you and be strengthened by the love and adoration of your people on this Palm Sunday.

34

*Then everyone shall be rescued
who calls on the name of the
LORD.*

Joel 3:5

Image: **The Seagull**

Last year while fishing at the seashore my line
got twisted around the wing of a seagull. He
was very agitated so I pulled him gently toward
me and let him fasten his beak on my knuckle.
This seemed to pacify him, enabling me to un-
wind the line from his wing with my other
hand. He was peaceful so long as he had
something to hold on to. We all need someone
to hold on to, but that need is not always
perceived clearly by the people around us.

Jesus is with us in all of our victories and
our defeats. When we are at the very bottom of
the well—lonely, hurting and approaching
despair—if we will reach out our hand in the
dark, Jesus will grasp it with love and strength
and assurance. He is there at the bottom of
every lonely, dark place loving us, simply
waiting for us to reach out in the dark to him.

Prayer:

Lord, you know how long the nights can be.
You sit beside me in the lonely hours and I

sometimes do not see you or hear you.

Give me the grace to know that you are there, always with me. Give me the grace to touch your spirit in love and receive your healing. Soften my hard and frightened heart and let your living waters of forgiveness and peace rush in to fill my emptiness.

35

Near the cross of Jesus there stood his mother, his mother's sister, Mary the wife of Clopas, and Mary Magdalene.

John 19:25

Image: Communication

Do you remember as a small child being very sick and in bed—perhaps with a high fever? Do you remember how comforting it was when your mother or dad sat by your bed and simply held your hand? No words were necessary. That experience can be soul-satisfying even for an adult.

There are times when words are inadequate, when they seem trivial compared to the thoughts and emotions we want to convey. Unfortunately, we sometimes mumble on, hoping that by the very number of words and the rapidity of speaking we can tell what is in our heart.

God in his generosity has given us ways of communicating which are more eloquent than words. How much tender love is expressed by a wife simply laying her hand on her husband's shoulder? How much understanding and compassion is revealed through the eyes of love?

Can any words express loyalty as fully as the friend who simply stands by, who is there?

Perhaps that is our vocation—to be in spirit and in mind always at the foot of the cross —simply to be there with Christ.

Prayer:

Jesus, you knew me before I was born; you were there at the moment of my birth. You are with me all the day long. If I awake in the night you are there. At the moment of death I know that you will be with me.

But I am with you too often, only in my fears, in my distress and in my needs. Teach me, Lord, to be with you always—in every situation—at every moment.

36

*"Be constantly on the watch! Stay
awake! You do not know when
the appointed time will come."*
                        Mark 13:33

Image: Watching

I was sitting in the sun enjoying a good book.
After a while I raised my head to take a
momentary break and my eyes swept lazily over
the patio. I was somewhat startled to see a
beautiful, almost transparent, tiny green lizard
just a few feet away staring at me intently. He
was motionless and must have been there for
some time.

   The intent, watchful eyes of that delicate
little creature reminded me that we are all being watched by someone infinitely great—God
who is always there, always with us, always
watching. His faithfulness, love and protection
are exercised in a continuum—never faltering,
never fading, never changing. His love and care
are infinite and beyond change or diminution.
God's love sometimes seems to change as we
move further away or closer to his law and to
his love. When we become lukewarm in our
love or disobedient to his law, our guilt makes
us feel alienated, far away.

God is and remains close. He is within us. His love is an ever-present reality, an eternal flame in our breast. We feel the warmth and power of that love in a special way when we are attending to him, when we are open and listening—truly, when we are watching him as he watches us.

Prayer:

Lord, there is nothing in my life that is hidden from your eyes. Every sin, every weakness, every virtuous act is clear and distinctly present to you. You know my needs before they occur. You know my prayers before I say them. I am totally under your loving eye and divine power.

You send your grace to aid me. You send the wisdom and knowledge of your Spirit to enlighten me. Lord, I want to respond always with vigor and courage to your call so that when death comes—suddenly or slowly—I am unashamedly ready to see the face of my God.

37

*Gracious is the L*ORD *and just;*
    yes, our God is merciful.
*The L*ORD *keeps the little ones;*
    I was brought low and he
        saved me.

                            Psalm 116:5-6

Image: The New Skates

As a child will do, I gave the wheel of my new
roller skates a spin and marveled at the sound,
the smooth hum, and the length of time the
spinning went on. As the wheel slowed down, I
gave it another spin and it accelerated and went
on spinning. I was fascinated at how well the
ball bearings functioned in their light coat of
oil.

God has made us something like that skate
wheel. When we yield to his hand through sub-
mission to his law and love and actively open
ourselves to his working in us, we spin
smoothly. We know from medical science and
other branches of learning that we are made
with infinite and exquisite precision and that
when we cooperate with nature and grace
things go well. When we rebel, we are penal-
ized.

In the physical order, that is easy to see. If

we eat too much, we get sick; if we stare at the sun, we damage our eyes. In the moral order, we can also see the penalties for violating God's law. Sometimes the penalties are not immediate, but they come with inevitability.

Close your eyes and see and hear that new, shiny skate wheel spinning smoothly in a little boy's hands. That is the way God wants you to be, functioning smoothly according to his law and love. And if we slow down or falter, his divine hand will give us that boost of grace to keep us spinning, to see us through.

Prayer:

Dear Lord, my heart is filled with love and gratitude for your sacrifice on Calvary. I thirst to see you, to tell you of my joy in your life.

Your grace gives me knowledge, words and strength that can only come from you alone. I feel your presence. I rest in your love, Jesus; keep me ever close to you.

38

This we know: our old self was crucified with him so that the sinful body might be destroyed and we might be slaves to sin no longer.

Romans 6:6

Image: Crucifixion

I prayed, and in my mind and spirit I seemed to be in Jerusalem the day they crucified Christ. I was at the scene. It was not like the pictures or tableaux that are shown. It was awful—hot, crowded, smelly, and no one sensing what was really happening. The Roman soldiers simply wanted to get it over with.

Jesus was hanging there in the blazing sun, slumped with fatigue, the nails tearing into his flesh, but worst of all, he couldn't breathe and his lungs were rapidly filling with fluid.

I felt a vague but uncontrollable desire to help him, to do something. I took a ladder and placed it against the crossarm of the crucifix and climbed up until I was on a level with his head. He turned his head slowly and looked at me with eyes glazed with pain and fatigue. I said, "Lord, do you know me?"

He said slowly and painfully as he gasped

for breath, "Of course, I know you. I am dying for you."

Prayer:

Jesus, son of David, have mercy on me. Jesus, son of God, hear my prayer. Lord, I know that in your eternal divine life you are eternally crucified and eternally risen. Give me the grace to hang on the cross with you today through prayer, fasting and sacrifice so that I may one day rise with you and reign with you forever in heaven.

39

*Yes, God so loved the world
that he gave his only Son.*

John 3:16

Image: Innocence Crucified

Bill had watched his eight-year-old daughter die
slowly and in pain. In his anger he questioned
the goodness and mercy of God.

He was a good man and so devoted to God
and the church that I desperately wanted to say
something healing and upbuilding to him. I
really couldn't until the day I knelt before a
crucifix and in my mind's eye saw an image of
God the Father looking down on Calvary.

I talked with Bill about how each of us
could visualize giving up his own life for someone, but that deliberately sending our own child
to die was unthinkable. How could God the
Father have put his only begotten son, Jesus,
through all of that pain and death for us, as sinful and unworthy as we are?

We talked about Jesus on the cross innocent
and blameless in his suffering and pain. About
how he died to show us not only that he loves
us but that no matter how deep our pain and
suffering or the pain of those we love, he shares
fully in it. He has been there.

Jesus, living outside of time, is eternally crucified. He is a now God, eternally crucified, eternally risen. He shows us that pain and suffering are a part of life that is not alien to him and should not be alien to us. We all have to take up our cross daily and follow him.

The image of the suffering and compassionate Jesus brought the gift of tears for Bill and the knowledge that opened the door to reconciliation with God.

Prayer:

Father God, what can I say to you in thanks? What gift can I offer you? What can I do to recognize in some way the awesome gift of your son?

I can pray. I can fast. I can sacrifice voluntarily. And I can accept involuntary sacrifice cheerfully. I can work to root out sin in my life. But none of these acts can repay your love. I accept my salvation with love and gratitude.

Images of God

40

*"It was not you who chose me,
it was I who chose you."*

John 15:16

Image: **Invitation**

It was mid-afternoon and I was alone in the
church among all the empty pews. I rested in
the deep silence. My eyes closed and I saw an
image of myself standing at the bottom of a
flight of stairs. I looked up and there was Jesus
on the upper landing. He was radiantly
transfigured and he beckoned to me to come up.

I was assailed by a welter of conflicting
thoughts and emotions. I had a great sense of
unworthiness, of my own sinfulness, of shame
and guilt. I also had a strong sensing of the
need for more time to prepare myself. The sud-
denness of the call seemed to be more than I
could adjust to. I simply wanted more time.

The ground I stood on seemed so safe and
familiar. I had a deep insecurity and fear about
leaving it. "You're not worthy; you're not ready;
you're not able to go to him," a voice seemed to
be saying. I suddenly realized that I was experiencing all of the weaknesses and fears of the
flesh, all at once. I also realized that going up
those stairs would not happen swiftly; it was a

life's work. I noticed a handrail on the wall, a sign of God's grace and help.

In my reverie, I carefully placed my foot on the first step, grasped the handrail and began to climb. Suddenly I knew in my heart that the seed of victory over sin and death was contained in that first step. I had only to believe, to be faithful and to persevere.

I felt a tremendous apostolic ache to share that knowledge and feeling with every man and woman on earth, to call them to look up, to rise, to ascend to that same Jesus who beckons them so lovingly.

Prayer:

Jesus, you went to the cross for me. In your human nature, you shrank from the torture and pain that awaited you. I am grateful that you understand my fears and hesitancy, my weakness—yes, even my panic—at surrendering all my earthly affections to you.

Help me, Lord, to let go, to abandon anyone or anything that keeps me apart from your love and will. Lord, draw me closer to you each day. Thank you for your victory!